MW01681223

The 60-Minute Identity Protection Plan

Close the doors most attackers rely on — in about an hour.

The 60-Minute Identity Protection Plan

Published by First Advantage Press

ISBN: 979-8-9962725-1-8

This book is provided for general informational and educational purposes only. It does not constitute legal, financial, tax, or other professional advice, and it is not a substitute for consultation with a qualified professional. While care has been taken to ensure accuracy, the publisher assumes no responsibility for errors or omissions, or for outcomes resulting from the use of this information. Web addresses, phone numbers, and procedures referenced may change over time.

First Advantage Press | Publishers of Self-Help and How-To Books | Founded March 2008

FIRSTADVANTAGEPRESS
Publishers of Self-Help and How-To Books

Contents

FOREWORD

The New Rules of Identity Theft

Something changed in April 2026.

Anthropic, one of the world's leading artificial intelligence companies, developed a new AI model and then made an almost unheard-of decision: they refused to release it to the public. The reason was straightforward. Their own tests showed the model could find weaknesses in virtually every major computer system and web browser—and break in—entirely on its own, with no human help.

That is not a distant corporate problem. It is a turning point for every one of us who banks online, checks email, or has a Social Security number.

Identity theft is not new. What is new is who—or what—is now doing it, and how fast. Everything that happened before April 2026 was child's play by comparison.

Why This Matters to You Personally

You may be thinking: I'm not a big company. Why would anyone come after me?

Here is the honest answer: because you're easier. Criminals have always preferred the path of least resistance. AI simply makes that path faster and cheaper to walk. A single attacker using today's AI tools can target thousands of ordinary people—not instead of corporations, but in addition to them—for almost no cost.

Your identity today is far more than your Social Security number. It is your bank login, your email account, the passwords your phone has memorized, the accounts that all share the same recovery address. Lose control of one, and the rest can fall quickly.

The capabilities Anthropic's researchers documented do not stay locked away forever. Similar tools will emerge—some already are. And when technology like that reaches the wrong hands, the fraudsters gain both reach and speed of access to your privacy and identity assets that simply did not exist before.

In Chapter 1, we describe some of the scenarios that could play out as a result of this shift—changes that alter the game in both scale and speed.

Not If. When.

Cybersecurity professionals have a saying they no longer consider controversial: it is no longer a question of whether you will be targeted. It is a question of when.

That used to apply mainly to large organizations. It applies to individuals now too.

People who have had their identity stolen spend an average of hundreds of hours over months—sometimes years—sorting out the damage: disputing accounts, contacting agencies, explaining to lenders what happened. The financial losses are real. So is the stress.

The good news is that protecting yourself does not require technical knowledge or expensive services. It requires about an hour of your time and a handful of decisions.

One Hour. One Decision.

This book was written with one promise: the core steps that will meaningfully protect you can be understood and put in place in approximately sixty minutes.

These steps will not make you invulnerable—nothing will. But they will close the doors that most attackers rely on. They will put you in a fundamentally different—and safer—category than most people who have never taken them. Start now. *— First Advantage Press*

PART I
Prevent

Reducing the Odds Before Anything Happens

CHAPTER 1

The New Threat Landscape

Several Factors That Increase the Probability You'll Be a Victim

THE RISK

For decades, the primary defense against phishing emails and phone scams was simple: they were easy to spot. Misspelled words, broken grammar, generic greetings, obvious urgency— "DEAR VALUED CUSTOMER YOUR ACCOUNT HAS BEEN COMPROMISED." A reasonably attentive person could identify a scam in seconds. That era is over.

Voice cloning has crossed the same threshold. With as little as three seconds of audio—a voicemail you left, a video you posted, a recording from a family event—AI can replicate your voice convincingly enough to deceive your spouse, your children, or your bank's phone representative. Fraudsters have already used this technology to impersonate family members in distress, demanding emergency wire transfers. They have used it to bypass voice authentication systems at financial institutions.

THE LOSS

The financial losses are significant. The Federal Trade Commission reported that American consumers lost over $12.5 billion to fraud in 2024, with identity theft accounting for more than 1.1 million of the nearly 6.5 million consumer reports filed. And those are only the cases that get reported.

> *The FTC received more than 1.1 million identity theft reports in 2024. Total fraud losses reached $12.5 billion—a significant increase over prior years. — FTC Consumer Sentinel Network Data Book, 2024 [1]*

But the financial loss is only part of the picture. Consider what identity theft means in practice. It means discovering that someone has opened seven credit accounts in your name and run them to the limit before you noticed. It means a mortgage denied at the worst possible moment because your credit score dropped 200 points without your knowledge. It means spending hundreds of hours on hold with credit bureaus, financial institutions, the Social Security Administration, and government agencies. That is not a weekend project. That is weeks of your life.

> *Victims spend an average of 200+ hours on recovery, including filing reports, disputing accounts, and rebuilding credit. — ITRC 2024 Consumer Impact Report [2]*

THE SOLUTION

The best offense is a good defense, and this 60-Minute Identity Protection Plan is a set of structural defenses that reduce your exposure. You can limit the damage when a breach occurs and accelerate your recovery when it does.

The chapters that follow walk through each layer of that plan. None of them require technical expertise. All of them require action. The combination of all five layers is what creates genuine protection. Doing one or two and stopping is the same mistake people have always made—and the attackers are very good at finding that one hole in your defense.

CHAPTER 2

Surface Area Reduction

You Cannot Protect What You Cannot See

THE RISK

Every piece of personally identifiable information that exists about you in a publicly accessible or commercially available database is a potential attack vector. Your name, address, phone number, date of birth, employer, relatives' names, vehicle information, property records—all of it is aggregated, bought, sold, and re-sold by a data broker industry that operates almost entirely outside of public awareness.

There are over 4,000 data broker companies in the United States. Most people have never heard of one. Yet these companies hold detailed profiles on virtually every American adult—profiles that are available for purchase by anyone willing to pay. Criminals use these profiles to construct the foundation of an identity theft campaign: they know where you live, who your family members are, where you bank, and what your daily patterns look like before they ever contact you.

The assumption that your information is private because you are "careful" is almost certainly false. If you have ever filled out a warranty card, signed up for a loyalty program, used a mobile app, purchased anything online, voted in an election, or owned property—your data is out there. Not some of it. Most of it.

> *Major data brokers hold databases covering hundreds of millions of Americans. Radaris alone maintains 183 million unique names and 594 million records. The industry encompasses more than 4,000 U.S. companies. — OneRep Industry Analysis, 2024 [4]*

THE LOSS

A large surface area means attackers arrive pre-armed. They know enough about you to craft a convincing attack before you have any warning. They can answer your security questions. They can pass the "knowledge-based authentication" challenges that banks use to verify identity—questions like "What street did you grow up on?" or "What was the name of your first pet?"—because that information is already in a database somewhere.

This is not a hypothetical. Security researchers have repeatedly demonstrated that most knowledge-based authentication questions can be answered using publicly available data within minutes. What felt like a security layer was, for many people, no security at all.

THE SOLUTION

Surface area reduction means systematically removing your information from the places it shouldn't be and containing it in the places it needs to be. Practically, this means:

- Submit opt-out requests to major data brokers—companies like Spokeo, Whitepages, BeenVerified, Intelius, and others. Paid services can automate these opt-outs across hundreds of brokers at once, or you can submit them yourself for free.
- Use a dedicated email address for financial accounts that is never used for retail, social media, or any public-facing purpose.
- Review your social media privacy settings and remove or restrict anything that answers common security questions—hometown, birthdate, family member names, pet names, employer history.
- Use a P.O. box or mail forwarding service for any correspondence you don't want tied to your home address.

None of this makes you invisible. The data that already exists cannot be fully recalled. However, automated opt-out services can find and remove much of your online presence from search engines and data brokers. Reducing your ongoing digital footprint matters—it slows the accumulation of fresh data, makes you a harder target than the next person, and deprives AI systems of the raw material they need to construct convincing attacks.

Do This Now

□ Opt out of the major data brokers or use a paid service to automate it.

□ Create a separate email address used only for financial accounts.

□ Tighten social-media privacy; remove hometown, birthdate, and family and pet names.

CHAPTER 3

Access Control

The Front Door to Your Entire Life

THE RISK

Your email account is not just an email account. It is the master key to everything else in your life. Your bank accounts, investment accounts, insurance policies, government records, and social media all have one thing in common: if you forget your password, you reset it via email. Which means that whoever controls your email controls your identity.

Password reuse is the single most exploited vulnerability in consumer identity security. The mechanics are straightforward: a criminal purchases a list of usernames and passwords leaked in a prior data breach—these lists sell for as little as a few dollars on the dark web—then systematically tests those credentials against hundreds of popular websites. This is called "credential stuffing," and it is almost entirely automated.

If you have used the same password on two different sites in the last decade, there is a meaningful probability that both credentials have been tested against your email account, your bank, and your investment accounts. Whether an attacker succeeded depends on how widely that combination was exposed—something you may have no way of knowing.

> *81% of hacking-related data breaches are caused by weak or reused passwords. — Verizon Data Breach Investigations Report [5]*

THE LOSS

Email account compromise is typically the first step in a cascading identity attack. Once an attacker is inside your email, they don't announce themselves. They read quietly. They identify your financial institutions from statement emails. They note your full name, address, and account numbers. They observe your communication patterns and the language you use.

Then they begin systematically resetting passwords for financial accounts—using the email account they already control to receive the reset links.

> *By the time most victims notice something is wrong, the attacker has had hours or days of undetected access. The damage done in that window can take years to undo.*

THE SOLUTION

Three actions close the vast majority of access control risk:

- Use a reputable password manager. Generate a unique, random password for every account. Never reuse.
- Enable multi-factor authentication (MFA) on every financial account, your email, and any account with access to sensitive data. Authenticator apps (Google Authenticator, Authy) are more secure than SMS-based codes, which can be intercepted through SIM-swapping attacks.
- Audit your email account's recovery options. Remove old phone numbers, outdated backup emails, and any recovery questions. These are attack surfaces.

> *If an attacker owns your email, they own your identity. Protect it accordingly.*

Do This Now

□ Install a password manager and replace reused passwords, financial accounts first.

□ Turn on multi-factor authentication everywhere—use an authenticator app, not SMS.

□ Remove old recovery phone numbers and backup emails from your accounts.

CHAPTER 4

Financial Containment

Assume You Will Be Breached. Limit the Damage.

THE RISK

Prevention is valuable. Containment is essential. The most well-defended individual is still vulnerable to a breach at an institution they trust—a bank, a hospital, a credit bureau, a government agency. The Equifax breach of 2017 exposed the Social Security numbers, birthdates, and addresses of 147 million Americans. The National Public Data breach of 2024 reportedly exposed the sensitive personal information of nearly every American adult. These were not the result of anything the victims did wrong.

When your data exists in a system you don't control, you cannot prevent it from being exposed in that system's breach. What you can control is how much damage a criminal can do once they have your information.

> *A credit freeze is free, takes 15 minutes, and stops new account fraud completely. Most people still haven't done it.*

THE LOSS

Without financial containment, a single breach can cascade into a multi-front assault. New credit accounts opened in your name. Loans taken out. Your existing accounts accessed and drained. Tax fraud filed in your name before you have a chance to submit your own return. Medical identity theft—someone receiving care under your name and insurance—which can corrupt your medical records and leave you with bills for treatments you never received.

Each of these requires a different recovery process. Each involves different institutions, different forms, different timelines. A victim dealing with all of them simultaneously can easily spend a year in active recovery—while the financial and credit consequences affect every major decision in their life.

THE SOLUTION

- Freeze your credit at all three major bureaus—Equifax, Experian, and TransUnion. A freeze prevents any new credit from being opened in your name without your explicit unfreezing action. It is free, reversible, and the single most effective tool against new account fraud.
- Consider also freezing at secondary bureaus—ChexSystems (used by banks for checking account applications), LexisNexis, and Innovis.
- Separate your financial accounts by purpose. Maintain one account for daily spending, a

separate one for savings, and never link them in ways that create single points of failure.

- Place a fraud alert with the credit bureaus if you suspect your information has been exposed. A fraud alert requires lenders to take extra steps to verify your identity before extending credit.

Do This Now

- □ Freeze your credit at Equifax, Experian, and TransUnion—it's free.
- □ Add freezes at ChexSystems, LexisNexis, and Innovis.
- □ Place a fraud alert if you suspect your information has been exposed.

CHAPTER 5

Home Title Fraud

The Crime That Could Cost You Everything You've Built

THE RISK

Most people have never heard of home title fraud. That is part of why it works.

Your home's title is a public record. In most jurisdictions, property records are maintained by county recorder offices and accessible to anyone. The process of transferring a property title—recording a deed—requires documentation and a notary, but it does not typically require the homeowner's presence or real-time verification.

What this means in practice is that a criminal who has sufficient personal information about you can forge a deed, have it notarized using a fraudulent or corrupt notary, and record a transfer of your property title to themselves or to a shell entity they control. This has happened to homeowners across the country—often to people who own their homes free and clear, because those properties are more attractive targets. No mortgage means no lender watching the title.

Vacant properties, rental properties, and paid-off homes are the highest-risk targets. FBI Special Agent Vivian Barrios: "Our elderly population… they are more likely to own homes without any mortgages on them. Because those have the biggest benefit to the criminal actor." — FBI Boston Division, April 2025 [6]

THE LOSS

Once a fraudulent deed is recorded, the criminal can use it to take out a mortgage against your property, sell the property to an unsuspecting buyer, or simply create enough legal confusion to hold the asset hostage while litigation plays out.

Here is what recovery looks like: you hire a real estate attorney. You file suit to quiet title—a legal action that asks the court to determine the true ownership of the property. This process takes months to years. It costs tens of thousands of dollars in legal fees. During that period, you may not be able to sell the property, refinance it, or use it as collateral. If a fraudulent mortgage was placed on it, you may be dealing with a lender who claims a lien on your home based on a loan you never took.

In the most severe cases—particularly when a fraudulent sale to a third party has been completed—recovering clear title can be extraordinarily difficult. Courts apply protections to bona fide purchasers who bought in good faith. You can find yourself in a legal dispute over your own home against someone who had nothing to do with the fraud.

> *From 2019 to 2023, more than 58,000 Americans reported $1.3 billion in real estate fraud losses to the FBI. Seniors represented 19% of complainants but suffered 44% of the financial losses. — FBI IC3 / FBI Boston Division Warning, April 2025 [6]*

The FBI and Federal Trade Commission have both issued warnings about the rising frequency of deed fraud. Major cities including New York, Philadelphia, Houston, and Los Angeles have created dedicated task forces to address it. After investigative reports aired in Massachusetts, every county registry of deeds now allows homeowners to sign up for free property recording alerts.

THE SOLUTION

- Set up property alerts through your county recorder's office. Many counties now offer free notifications when any document is recorded against your property. This is the most direct early-warning system available.
- Consider home title lock services that offer monitoring and alert services specifically for property title changes. These do not prevent fraud, but they detect it early, which is critical.

- Review your property records annually. Log in to your county assessor or recorder website and confirm that the ownership record matches what you expect.
- If you own investment properties or vacant land—properties you may not actively monitor—increase the review frequency. These are the highest-risk assets.
- Title insurance from your original purchase provides some protection, but it typically covers conditions at the time of purchase. Ask your insurance provider specifically about post-purchase fraud protection.

The window between when fraud is committed and when it is discovered is the most dangerous period. The longer the fraud goes undetected, the more complicated and expensive the recovery becomes. Early detection is not just helpful—it is the difference between a problem and a catastrophe.

Do This Now

□ Sign up for free property-recording alerts at your county recorder's office.

□ Review your property record once a year to confirm ownership.

□ Ask your title insurer about coverage for post-purchase fraud.

CHAPTER 6

Behavioral Awareness

Technology Can't Save You If Your Behavior Is Predictable

THE RISK

Even the best security measures can fail in a single moment of human compliance. Attackers understand this, which is why so many sophisticated fraud schemes create urgency: "Your account will be closed in 24 hours," "There is a warrant for your arrest," or "Your grandson has been in an accident." Urgency shuts down critical thinking.

AI has made urgency-based attacks dramatically more effective because it has eliminated the signals that used to identify them. The grammar is perfect. The voice sounds exactly like your bank. The email has the right logo, the right formatting, and the right account number—because it was built using your actual data. The only tell left is the urgency itself, and even that is now calibrated to feel appropriate.

> *Impostor scams—where criminals pose as trusted entities to create urgency—were the top-reported fraud category in 2024, with more than 847,000 complaints. — FTC Consumer Sentinel Network Data Book 2024 [7]*

THE LOSS

Behavioral attacks succeed against educated, careful, security-conscious people every day. A CFO wires funds to a fraudulent account after receiving what appears to be an urgent email from the CEO—this is called Business Email Compromise, and it costs businesses billions annually. A retiree sends gift cards to a "Social Security Administration officer" who threatens arrest. An adult child wires emergency bail money to someone impersonating a grandchild using an AI-cloned voice.

> *These are not failures of intelligence. They are failures of protocol—the absence of a personal policy for how to respond to urgent financial requests.*

THE SOLUTION

Build simple personal protocols and follow them without exception:

- Any unexpected communication requesting financial action requires a second-channel verification. If your "bank" calls you, hang up and call the number on the back of your card. If your "grandson" calls from an unknown number, call his actual phone number before responding.
- Treat urgency itself as a red flag. Legitimate institutions do not require you to act within hours. The more urgency being applied, the more skepticism is warranted.

- Establish a family code word for emergency situations. If a family member calls in distress, the code word confirms identity. AI-cloned voices cannot know a code word established in advance.
- Never act on links or attachments in unexpected emails. Navigate directly to the institution's website by typing the address yourself.

Do This Now

- □ Set a family code word for emergencies.
- □ Verify any urgent money request on a second channel—hang up and call the number you know.
- □ Treat urgency itself as the warning sign.

CHAPTER 7

Monitoring & Detection

You Can't Stop Everything. You Must Detect Early.

THE RISK

Even with every protective layer in place, breaches happen. Institutions you trust get compromised. Old data resurfaces. A sophisticated attack finds a gap. The question is not whether you will ever be a victim—the question is how quickly you will know, and how fast you will respond.

Identity theft is often discovered quickly when it involves an existing credit card or bank account, but more complex forms—such as new-account fraud, tax identity theft, medical identity theft, or synthetic identity fraud—can go undetected for months or longer. During that time, criminals may open accounts, seek credit, file fraudulent tax returns, obtain medical services, or create records that can take significant time and effort to correct.

THE LOSS

Late detection is not just an inconvenience—it is a compounding liability. Every fraudulent account that ages becomes a larger debt. Every month of tax fraud complicates the IRS dispute process. Every medical record corrupted by an impersonator is a record that could affect your actual medical care. The damage done in month twelve of an undetected breach is qualitatively different from the damage done in week one.

> *FTC research shows that when fraud is discovered within five months, losses remain under $5,000 in 82% of cases. When discovery takes six months or more, losses exceed $5,000 in 44% of cases. Speed of detection is the single greatest determinant of recovery cost. — FTC Historical Data, via BitsFromBytes 2026 [8]*

THE SOLUTION

- Enable real-time transaction alerts on every financial account. Most banks and credit card companies offer push notifications for any transaction over a threshold you set. Set it to zero. Know about every transaction.
- Monitor your credit reports actively. All three bureaus are required by law to provide a free report annually at AnnualCreditReport.com. Stagger your requests—one bureau every four months—to maintain year-round coverage.
- Use a credit monitoring service that provides real-time alerts for new accounts, inquiries, and changes to your credit file. Many banks offer this as a free benefit.
- Review your Social Security earnings record annually at ssa.gov to detect any unauthorized use of your SSN for employment purposes.

Do This Now

- □ Turn on transaction alerts on every account and set the threshold to zero.
- □ Stagger your free credit reports—one bureau every four months.
- □ Check your Social Security earnings record each year at ssa.gov.

CHAPTER 8

The Recovery Process

What It Really Costs—And Why Most People Aren't Ready

The Honest Picture

Nobody talks honestly about what recovering from identity theft involves. Government agencies that track it describe the process in bureaucratic language that obscures the human reality. So here it is plainly.

the ITRC's 2024 report, nearly half of victims who contacted ITRC said their issue was **not yet resolved**, and 10% reported dealing with the incident for **six months to one year**. Older FTC research found average resolution time of **30 hours overall** and **60 hours** for more serious new-account/other-fraud cases. [2,3]

During that period, you will spend dozens to hundreds of hours on the phone, writing letters, filing disputes, and following up on disputes that have gone nowhere. You will be asked to provide the same documentation to ten different institutions. Some of them will lose it. You will provide it again.

> *The process is designed for institutions, not for victims. Nobody is managing it for you.*

The Specific Steps Nobody Prepares You For

Step one is filing a report. You file a report with the FTC at IdentityTheft.gov, which generates an Identity Theft Report—a document you will need for virtually every subsequent step. You may also need to file a police report with your local jurisdiction, which some creditors require before they will remove fraudulent accounts.

Step two is placing a fraud alert or credit freeze at all three bureaus—if you haven't already done this preventively, you're doing it now in response to active fraud. This stops new damage, but it does not undo what has already been done.

Step three is disputing fraudulent accounts. You contact each creditor that has a fraudulent account in your name. You send the Identity Theft Report, a copy of your police report, proof of identity, and a written dispute letter. Under the Fair Credit Reporting Act, creditors are required to investigate and respond within 30 days. Some comply. Many drag the process out. Some will close the account; others will ask for more documentation. A few will initially deny your dispute and require you to escalate.

Step four is working with the credit bureaus directly. Even after a creditor removes a fraudulent account from their records, the entry may persist on your credit report. You file separate disputes with each bureau—Equifax,

Experian, and TransUnion—for each fraudulent entry. Each dispute is handled separately. A removal from one bureau does not automatically remove it from the others.

> *Disputing a single fraudulent account across all three bureaus requires a minimum of 3–5 separate written communications per account. — FTC consumer guidance / ITRC 2024 [9]*

The Compounding Complications

Tax-related identity theft adds the IRS to the list of institutions you may need to work with. If someone files a fraudulent return using your Social Security number, the IRS may require you to verify your identity or file Form 14039, Identity Theft Affidavit. IRS identity-theft cases can take well over a year to resolve. To reduce future risk, taxpayers can obtain an IRS Identity Protection PIN, which must be used when filing federal tax returns.

Medical identity theft adds healthcare providers, insurance companies, and potentially your state insurance commissioner to the process. Correcting a corrupted medical record is particularly challenging because healthcare providers have specific HIPAA obligations that can complicate the correction process.

And home title fraud, as described in the previous chapter, adds real estate attorneys, courts, county recorder offices, and potentially mortgage lenders to a process that can extend for years and cost tens of thousands of dollars in legal fees—with no guarantee of outcome.

> *The ITRC's 2024 Consumer Impact Report found that 87% of identity theft victims reported feeling anxious or worried; 77% felt violated. The cumulative emotional weight of this process is real and lasting. [10]*

Recovery is not a single conversation. It is a part-time job that arrives without warning and doesn't end when you'd like it to.

The victims who navigate recovery most effectively share a common approach: they treat it like a project. They document everything—every call, every letter, every response, every reference number. They follow up every verbal commitment in writing. They escalate quickly when disputes are denied or ignored. And they use every resource available, including the Consumer Financial Protection Bureau's complaint portal, which has real authority over financial institutions and often produces results that direct disputes do not.

Services that specialize in identity theft recovery—whether through a dedicated service, an attorney who specializes in FCRA litigation, or an identity protection plan that includes recovery assistance—can meaningfully reduce the time and stress involved. They know the process. They know which escalation paths work. They know which institutions respond to which types of pressure. This expertise has real value.

CHAPTER 9

Your 60-Minute Protection Plan

Stop Reading. Start Doing.

Everything in this book is context. This chapter is action. If you do nothing else, do these five things—in this order—within the next hour. You will not be invulnerable. Nobody is. But you will be meaningfully more protected than you were before you started, and more protected than many adults who have read something like this, nodded thoughtfully, and done nothing.

Step 1 — Freeze Your Credit

Estimated time: 10 minutes

Go to equifax.com, experian.com, and transunion.com. Create an account at each and initiate a credit freeze. This is free by federal law. A freeze prevents any new credit from being opened in your name. It does not affect your existing accounts or your credit score. You can temporarily lift it when you need to apply for credit. Do this first because it is the single highest-impact action on this list.

- Equifax: equifax.com/personal/credit-report-services
- Experian: experian.com/freeze/center.html
- TransUnion: transunion.com/credit-freeze

Step 2 — Lock Down Your Primary Email Account

Estimated time: 15 minutes

Log into your primary email account. Change the password to something you have never used before—at least 16 characters or use a generated password if you have a password manager. Enable two-factor authentication using an authenticator app (not SMS if possible). Review and remove any old recovery email addresses or phone numbers that you no longer control.

- For Gmail: myaccount.google.com/security
- For Outlook: account.microsoft.com/security
- Authenticator apps: Google Authenticator or Authy (both free)

Step 3 — Install a Password Manager

Estimated time: 10 minutes

Set it up with a strong master password. Begin immediately by adding your financial accounts, replacing any reused passwords with generated ones. You do not need to convert every account in one session—start with what matters most.

- Priority accounts first: banking, investment, email, insurance

Step 4 — Enable Real-Time Financial Alerts

Estimated time: 10 minutes

Log into your bank and credit card accounts. Find the alerts or notifications section. Enable push notifications or email alerts for every transaction. Set the threshold to the lowest possible amount—ideally any transaction. Check your investment accounts for similar alert options.

- Every major bank now offers transaction alerts
- Set alerts on credit cards, checking, and savings accounts
- Consider also enabling login alerts for financial accounts

Step 5 — Set Up Property Monitoring and Data Broker Opt-Out

Estimated time: 15 minutes

Visit your county recorder or assessor's website and search for property alert notifications. Many counties offer free email alerts when any document is recorded against a specific property address.

- Search "[your county] property alert" to find your county's notification system
- optoutprescreen.com — opt out of prescreened credit offers
- donotcall.gov — register your phone number with the National Do Not Call Registry
- Remove your personal information from data broker and people-search directories. Instead of forcing you to hunt down and complete hundreds of individual opt-out forms yourself a paid removal service can do it across many brokers at once.

> *When you finish these five steps, you have closed more security gaps than most Americans have ever addressed. A small fraction of Americans has simultaneously frozen their credit, enabled MFA, used a password manager, set up financial alerts, AND established property monitoring. You are now in that group. — ITRC [11]*

Checkpoint: How Many Doors Are Still Open?

You've built your defenses. Before turning to Recovery, check every box still true of you.

- ☐ I reuse one password across several accounts.
- ☐ Some key accounts lack two-factor login.
- ☐ My credit isn't frozen at all three bureaus.
- ☐ I've never checked my home's title records.
- ☐ I've never opted out of data-broker sites.
- ☐ I have no active identity monitoring.
- ☐ I click links without checking the sender.
- ☐ I post private details on social media.
- ☐ I have old accounts I've never closed.
- ☐ I don't know my first move after a theft.

Count your checks.

0 — You're locked down. Stay alert.

1–3 — A few doors are open. Go back and close them.

More than 3 — You're holding the door open. Close these gaps before moving on — most take only minutes.

PART II

Recover

What To Do When It Happens Anyway

CHAPTER 10

When Prevention Fails

Prevention closes doors. This part assumes one got opened anyway.

Part I was about reducing the odds. This part assumes the odds caught up with you. Maybe a company you trusted was breached. Maybe a single convincing phone call got past you on a bad day. However it happened, the question now is not how it happened—that can wait. The question is how fast you act and how well you organize what comes next.

Here is the most important thing to understand before you do anything else: recovery is not a single phone call. It is a project. It has a beginning, a sequence of steps, and an end—but only if you treat it like a project. The victims who recover fastest and lose the least are not the ones who panic, and they are not the ones who freeze. They are the ones who move quickly in the first hours, document everything from the first minute, and follow up in writing on every promise anyone makes them.

> *Speed is leverage. The single biggest factor in how much identity theft costs you is how fast you catch it and how fast you respond. Every hour an attacker operates undetected is an hour of damage you will later have to undo.*

This chapter gives you the sequence. The next pages are organized the way the clock actually runs: the first hour, the first week, the first month. After that, a one-page emergency checklist you can act from directly, and then specific playbooks for the harder cases—new-account fraud, tax fraud, medical fraud, and home title fraud—because each of those drags a different set of institutions into the process.

The First Hour: Stop the Bleeding

The goal in the first hour is containment, not investigation. You are not trying to understand the full scope of what happened. You are trying to shut off the attacker's access and freeze your exposure before more damage is done. Do these in order.

1. Start a log. Open a notebook or a document and write down the date and time you discovered the problem. From this moment, record every call you make, every person you speak to, every reference or case number you are given, and every promise made to you. This log is the single most valuable tool you have. You will reference it for months.
2. Secure the compromised account first. If you know which account was breached—email, bank, or otherwise—change its password to something entirely new, turn on multi-factor authentication, and sign out all other active sessions. If it is your email, do this before anything else, because your email is the reset key to everything else.

3. Call the fraud line of any financial institution involved. Use the number printed on the back of your card or your statement—never a number from an email or text. Report the unauthorized activity and ask them to flag the account. Debit cards and credit cards carry different protections and different deadlines, and reporting quickly is what preserves them.
4. Freeze your credit at all three bureaus. If you did this preventively in Part I, you are ahead. If not, do it now at Equifax, Experian, and TransUnion. It is free, and it stops new accounts from being opened while you sort out the rest.
5. Place a fraud alert. One call to any one of the three bureaus places an alert with all three. An initial fraud alert lasts one year and tells lenders to take extra steps to verify identity before extending credit.
6. File your report at IdentityTheft.gov. The Federal Trade Commission's site walks you through a series of questions and generates an Identity Theft Report and a personalized recovery plan. That report is the document nearly every other institution will ask you for. Get it early.

> *Report unauthorized debit transactions fast. Federal rules tie your maximum liability to how quickly you report: report within two business days and your exposure is capped at a low amount; wait longer and that cap rises sharply. Credit cards carry stronger protections than debit cards—another reason to route spending through credit.*

The First Week: Contain and Formalize

With the immediate bleeding stopped, the first week is about making everything official and notifying everyone who needs to know. Verbal reports are a start; written records are what hold up.

- File a police report if needed. Some creditors will not remove fraudulent accounts without one. Bring your FTC Identity Theft Report to the police station—together, the two documents form what is often called an Identity Theft Report, which unlocks specific legal rights described below.
- Notify every affected institution in writing. A phone call opens the case; a written notice creates the paper trail. Send notices to each bank, card issuer, or lender involved, reference your report, and keep copies of everything you send and the dates you sent it.
- Change passwords anywhere you reused the compromised one. If the breached password was used on other sites, assume those are exposed too. Replace each with a unique, generated password and enable multi-factor authentication.
- Request records of the fraud. Federal law gives identity theft victims the right to obtain business records related to fraudulent transactions made in their name. This helps you document the damage and can support your disputes.
- Decide between an extended fraud alert and a freeze. An extended fraud alert lasts seven years but requires an Identity Theft Report; a credit freeze gives stronger protection and is free. Many victims keep the freeze in place permanently and lift it only when applying for credit.

Everything in writing. If an institution tells you over the phone that an account will be closed or a charge reversed, follow up the same day with a short written message confirming what you were told, the date, and the name of the person you spoke with. Verbal commitments disappear; written ones do not.

The First Month and Beyond: Dispute and Repair

The first month is where the slow, grinding work happens: removing fraudulent accounts and entries, repairing your credit, and escalating when institutions stall. This is the part that tests patience, and it is where your log and your written records pay off.

- Dispute fraudulent accounts with each creditor. Send each creditor that has a fraudulent account a written dispute with your Identity Theft Report, proof of identity, and a clear statement that the account is not yours. Under the Fair Credit Reporting Act, they are generally required to investigate and respond within about 30 days—up to 45 days if you provide additional documents during the investigation or the dispute stems from your free annual report.
- Dispute fraudulent entries with each bureau separately. A fraudulent item can appear on one, two, or all three credit reports, and each bureau handles its own disputes. Removal from one does not remove it from the others. File with each.
- Use the block right. When information on your credit report results from identity theft, the bureaus must block it from appearing—no later than four business

days after you provide a valid Identity Theft Report, proof of identity, and identification of the items. This right, Section 605B of the Fair Credit Reporting Act, is underused and powerful; cite it by name.

- Escalate to the CFPB when creditors stall. The Consumer Financial Protection Bureau runs a complaint portal with real authority over financial institutions. Complaints filed there frequently produce results that direct disputes do not, and companies are expected to respond within a set window.
- Keep watching. Pull all three credit reports, confirm removed items stay removed, and watch for new fraud. Fraud rings often return to a name that paid off once.

Recovery rarely follows a straight line. Some institutions will respond promptly and professionally. Others will lose your documents, deny a valid dispute, or simply go quiet. Expect this, and treat each obstacle as a step in the project rather than a verdict on whether you will succeed. You will get through it—methodically, in writing, one institution at a time.

If It Happens to You: The Emergency Checklist

Use this page as a guide to track through the recovery process. If you ever discover fraud, work straight down this list.

Right now (the first hour)

- Start a written log—date, time, every call, every reference number.

- Change the password and turn on MFA for any compromised account—email first.
- Call the fraud line on the back of your card; report unauthorized activity.
- Freeze credit at Equifax, Experian, and TransUnion (free).
- Place a one-year fraud alert (one bureau notifies all three).
- File at IdentityTheft.gov and save your Identity Theft Report.

This week

- File a police report if a creditor requires one; bring your FTC report.
- Notify every affected institution in writing; keep copies.
- Replace any reused passwords; enable MFA broadly.
- Request records of the fraudulent transactions.

This month

- Dispute each fraudulent account with the creditor (about 30-day response window).
- Dispute each fraudulent entry with each bureau separately.
- Invoke the identity-theft block right to remove fraud-related items.
- Escalate stalled cases through the CFPB complaint portal.
- Re-pull all three reports and keep monitoring.

Recovery by Type

The checklist above handles the common case. But four kinds of identity theft pull in institutions of their own, with their own forms and timelines. If any of these apply to you, layer the steps here on top of the core sequence.

New-Account Fraud

This is the classic case: someone uses your information to open credit cards, loans, or utility accounts in your name. Beyond the core steps, your strongest tool is the block right. Once you give a credit bureau your Identity Theft Report, proof of identity, and identification of the fraudulent items, it must block that information from your report within four business days—and notify the furnisher that the debt may be the product of identity theft. Send each creditor a separate written dispute as well, because a removed credit-report entry does not erase the underlying account at the lender.

Tax Identity Theft

You usually discover this in one of two ways: your electronically filed return is rejected because a return has already been filed under your Social Security number, or you receive a notice from the IRS about a return you never filed. File IRS Form 14039, the Identity Theft Affidavit, and continue filing your real return—on paper if necessary. Contact the IRS through the channels listed on the notice you received. Once your case is resolved you are enrolled in the IRS Identity Protection PIN program automatically—but any taxpayer can opt in proactively at IRS.gov. The IP PIN is a six-digit number, reissued each calendar year, that must accompany your federal return and blocks anyone else from filing under your number. Be patient: IRS identity-theft cases can take many months to fully resolve.

Medical Identity Theft

This is when someone obtains medical care, prescriptions, or equipment using your identity or insurance. It is dangerous in two directions: it can leave you with bills and false claims, and it can corrupt your actual medical record in ways that affect your future care. Notify your health insurer's fraud department and request a list of recent claims. Ask each provider for an accounting of disclosures and use your right under federal health-privacy law to request corrections to records that contain another person's information. Watch your explanation-of-benefits statements the way you watch bank alerts.

Home Title Fraud

If a fraudulent deed has been recorded against your property, move quickly—delay is what turns this from a problem into a catastrophe. Confirm the current recorded owner through your county recorder or assessor. Report the fraud to the FBI's Internet Crime Complaint Center at IC3.gov and to local law enforcement. Retain a real estate attorney; the remedy is typically a quiet-title action asking a court to confirm true ownership, which can take months and real legal expense. Notify your title insurer and ask specifically about coverage for post-purchase fraud. The earlier you catch a fraudulent recording, the simpler and cheaper the cleanup.

> *One project, many fronts. A serious case can involve several of these at once. Do not try to hold it all in your head. Keep one master log, give each institution its own page, and work the list. Methodical beats frantic every time.*

PART III

The Toolkit

Field Guides, Tools, and Quick References

Case Files

The following are composites, drawn from patterns in commonly reported cases rather than any one real person, to show how these crimes actually unfold.

The 8 a.m. Phone Call

Joe, 71, answered and heard his grandson's voice—shaky, saying he'd been in a wreck and arrested out of state, begging him not to tell his parents. A “lawyer” took the phone and asked for $9,000 in gift cards for bail. Joe was halfway to the store before he remembered the family code word he'd set up that spring. He called his grandson's real number. His grandson was at work, fine. The voice had been cloned from a podcast interview posted online.

The Investment That Wasn't

A widow in her sixties met someone warm and patient through a messaging app. After two months he showed her a trading platform with steady, beautiful gains. She put in $40,000, watched it “grow,” and tried to withdraw for a roof repair. Suddenly there were “taxes” to pay first, then fees, then silence. The platform, the gains, and the man were all fabricated.

The Mortgage That Appeared

A retired couple owned their home free and clear. A county recording alert—one they'd set up in an afternoon—flagged a deed transfer they never authorized. A forged quitclaim deed had moved their title to a shell company that then sought a loan against the house. Because they caught it in days, their attorney untangled it in months instead of years.

The Refund Someone Else Claimed

A man went to e-file his return and it bounced: a return had already been filed under his Social Security number, and the refund was gone. He filed an Identity Theft Affidavit, submitted his real return on paper, and—once resolved—enrolled in an IRS Identity Protection PIN so it couldn't happen again.

The Breach That Snowballed

An old password, reused for years, surfaced in a data breach. An attacker used it to walk into an email account, sat quietly reading statements, then began resetting bank and brokerage passwords using that same inbox. The owner noticed only when a transaction alert—set to notify on every charge—fired for a purchase she didn't make. The alert, and a fast call to the bank, stopped it before the brokerage was drained.

Common Scams: A Field Guide

The fastest way to avoid a scam is to recognize its shape. Here are the ones doing the most damage right now, and the single tell that gives each one away.

The Family Emergency Call

How it works: A caller claims a grandchild or relative is in trouble—an accident, an arrest, a hospital—and needs money wired or sent as gift cards immediately. AI voice-cloning can make the voice sound exactly right.

Spot it: Hang up and call the relative directly, or ask for the family code word. Real emergencies survive a five-minute pause; scams do not.

Romance Into Investment ("Pig Butchering")

How it works: An attentive new online partner builds trust over weeks, then introduces a can't-miss crypto or trading platform showing fake gains until you try to withdraw.

Spot it: Never invest based on someone you've only met online, no matter how real the relationship feels.

Tech Support

How it works: A pop-up or cold call warns your computer is infected and offers to fix it—via remote access and a fee.

Spot it: Legitimate companies never cold-call about a virus. Close the window; don't call the number it shows.

Government Impersonation

How it works: A “caller from the IRS, Social Security, or police” threatens arrest, frozen benefits, or fines unless you pay right now, often in gift cards or crypto.

Spot it: Government agencies don't demand gift cards or threaten arrest by phone. It's a scam, every time.

The Bank “Fraud Department”

How it works: Someone posing as your bank says they've spotted fraud and asks you to “verify” details or move money to a “safe account.”

Spot it: Hang up and call the number on the back of your card. No real bank moves your money to keep it safe.

Phishing and Smishing

How it works: Emails or texts impersonate a bank, retailer, or delivery service with a link to “verify,” “pay a fee,” or “reschedule delivery.”

Spot it: Don't tap links in unexpected messages. Open the company's site yourself by typing the address.

The QR-Code Trap (“Quishing”)

How it works: A malicious QR code—on a flyer, a parking meter, or in an email—leads to a fake login or payment page.

Spot it: Treat a QR code like a link from a stranger. Don't scan one that asks you to log in or pay.

Frequently Asked Questions

Short answers to the questions readers ask most. For the full treatment, see the chapter noted in each answer.

Does freezing my credit hurt my credit score?

No. A freeze has no effect on your score. It simply stops new accounts from being opened in your name.

If I freeze my credit, can I still use my existing cards?

Yes. A freeze only blocks new credit. Your existing cards, loans, and accounts keep working normally.

Is a credit freeze the same as a "credit lock"?

No. A freeze is governed by federal law and is always free. "Locks" are bureau products that may carry their own terms or fees. Use the freeze.

Do I have to pay to freeze or unfreeze?

No. A federal law that took effect in 2018 made placing, lifting, and removing a freeze free at all three nationwide bureaus.

How is a fraud alert different from a freeze?

A fraud alert asks lenders to verify your identity before granting credit; a freeze blocks new credit outright. The freeze is the stronger tool. You can use both.

I've never been a victim—should I still freeze?

Yes. Anyone can freeze their credit at any time, for any reason. You don't have to wait to be harmed first.

What is the single most important step?

Freeze your credit at all three bureaus. It is free, fast, and the most effective single defense against new-account fraud (Chapter 4).

Is identity-theft insurance worth it?

It generally reimburses certain costs and provides recovery help; it does not prevent theft. Weigh its price against the free steps in this book, which do the prevention.

Are password managers safe?

A reputable password manager is far safer than reusing passwords. Protect it with a strong master password and multi-factor authentication (Chapter 3).

Should I use text-message codes or an authenticator app?

An authenticator app is more secure. Text-message codes can be intercepted through a SIM-swap attack (Chapter 3).

How often should I check my credit reports?

Stagger the free reports you're entitled to—pull one bureau every four months at AnnualCreditReport.com—or use a monitoring service (Chapter 7).

What should I do first if I think I've been hit?

Secure the compromised account, call your bank's fraud line, freeze your credit, and file at IdentityTheft.gov. The full sequence is in Part II.

Do I need to file a police report?

Sometimes. Certain creditors require one before removing fraudulent accounts. Bring your FTC Identity Theft Report when you file (Part II).

Should I freeze my child's credit?

If your child is under 16, yes. The process differs from an adult freeze; each bureau gives specific instructions. See "Who's Most at Risk."

Can someone steal a deceased relative's identity?

Yes—it's common enough to have a name, "ghosting." Acting quickly to notify the bureaus and agencies prevents it. See "Who's Most at Risk."

What is an IRS IP PIN, and should I get one?

It's a six-digit number, reissued yearly, that must be on your federal return and blocks anyone else from filing under your Social Security number. Any taxpayer can opt in at IRS.gov.

My information was already in a breach—is it too late?

No. You can't recall data that's already exposed, but the containment steps in this book limit how much damage anyone can do with it.

Will these steps make me completely safe?

Nothing makes anyone completely safe. These steps close the doors most attackers rely on and put you in a far safer category than people who do nothing.

Who's Most at Risk

The plan protects everyone, but four groups face sharper risks and need a few extra moves.

Protecting Seniors

Older Americans are the most-targeted group and absorb the heaviest losses—billions of dollars a year—because criminals combine isolation, trust, and the fact that many own paid-off homes. The common attacks are the grandparent emergency call, the "tech support" pop-up, government-impersonation threats, and slow-build romance and investment scams.

- Agree on a family code word so a cloned voice can't pass as a relative in distress.
- Freeze credit and set up county property-recording alerts—paid-off homes are prime title-fraud targets.
- Name a trusted contact, and make "I'll call you back" the default answer to any urgent money request.

Protecting Children and Teens

A child's Social Security number is a clean slate, which makes it valuable—and fraud against it can go undetected for years, often surfacing only when a teenager is denied a first job, loan, or apartment.

- Freeze your child's credit at all three bureaus; the process differs from an adult freeze, and each bureau gives instructions.
- Be sparing with your child's identifying details on forms, apps, and social media.

- If you ever receive credit offers or collection notices in a young child's name, treat it as a red flag and check for fraud.

After a Death: Preventing "Ghosting"

Criminals scan obituaries and use a deceased person's identity to open accounts and file returns—before the family thinks to lock things down. A few prompt notifications shut this off.

- Send a copy of the death certificate to all three credit bureaus and ask them to flag the file "deceased—do not issue credit."
- Notify the Social Security Administration, the IRS, banks, lenders, and insurers in writing.
- Request the deceased's credit reports to check for accounts that shouldn't exist.

Servicemembers and the Deployed

Deployment and frequent moves make monitoring harder, so the law gives servicemembers extra tools—use them.

- Place an active-duty alert, which tells lenders to verify identity and lasts one year (renewable for a deployment).
- Active-duty servicemembers and National Guard members can get free electronic credit monitoring from each of the three bureaus.
- Freeze your credit before a deployment; you can lift it remotely when you need it.

Copy-and-Use Templates

Three letters that do most of the heavy lifting in a recovery. Adapt the bracketed fields and send.

The templates below are built from the model letters the Federal Trade Commission makes available to the public. They are starting points, not legal advice—fill in the bracketed information, delete anything that does not apply, and keep a copy of everything you send. Three rules apply to all of them: send copies of your documents, never originals; mail anything important by certified mail with return receipt requested so you can prove it arrived; and address each letter to the company's current dispute address, which appears on your credit report or on the company's website, since these addresses change.

Template 1 — Dispute and Block Letter to a Credit Bureau

Use this to remove accounts or entries on your credit report that resulted from identity theft.

> [Your full name]
> [Your street address]
> [City, State ZIP]
>
> [Date]
>
> [Credit bureau name]
> [Bureau dispute address — from your credit report or the bureau's website]

Re: Request to block and remove information resulting from identity theft

To Whom It May Concern:

I am a victim of identity theft. The information listed below appears on my credit report and is the result of that theft. It does not relate to any transaction or account that I opened or authorized.

Under Section 605B of the Fair Credit Reporting Act (15 U.S.C. § 1681c-2), I request that you block this information from my credit file. As the law requires, I have enclosed a copy of my Identity Theft Report, proof of my identity, and identification of the specific items below.

Items resulting from identity theft:

• [Creditor / furnisher name, account number, amount, date]

• [Creditor / furnisher name, account number, amount, date]

Please block these items within four business days as required by law, notify the furnisher(s) that the information may be the result of identity theft, and confirm in writing when the block is complete.

Sincerely,

[Signature]

[Printed name]

Enclosures: copy of Identity Theft Report; copy of government-issued photo ID; copy of proof of address

Template 2 — Extended Fraud Alert Request

Use this to place a seven-year fraud alert in writing. (A one-year initial alert can be placed instantly by phone or online with any one bureau, which then notifies the other two.)

[Your full name]
[Your street address]
[City, State ZIP]

[Date]

[Credit bureau name]
[Bureau address]

Re: Request for an extended fraud alert

To Whom It May Concern:

I am a victim of identity theft and request that you place an extended fraud alert on my credit file for seven years, as provided under the Fair Credit Reporting Act. I have enclosed a copy of my Identity Theft Report and proof of my identity.

While this alert is in place, please:

- Contact me at the number(s) below before approving any new credit in my name; and
- Remove my name from prescreened credit and insurance offer lists for five years, unless I request otherwise.

Verification contact: [phone], [alternate phone].

Please confirm in writing that the alert has been placed.

Sincerely,

[Signature]
[Printed name]

Enclosures: copy of Identity Theft Report; copy of proof of identity

Template 3 — CFPB Complaint

Use this when a bank, lender, or credit bureau has stalled or refused a valid dispute. File online at consumerfinance.gov/complaint; the Consumer Financial Protection Bureau forwards it to the company and tracks the response, which generally arrives within about 15 days.

A CFPB complaint is an online form, not a mailed letter. Prepare the fields below, then paste your narrative into the "what happened" box. Keep it factual and short, and attach your prior dispute letter and any response you received.

Company: [name of the bank, lender, or credit bureau]
Product / service: [e.g., credit reporting; credit card; checking account]
Issue: [e.g., incorrect information on report; fraud or identity theft]
Dates and amounts: [as applicable]

What happened (paste this, edited to fit):

On [date] I discovered that [company] is reporting a [account type] opened in my name that I did not open or authorize. I am a victim of identity theft and filed an FTC Identity Theft Report on [date] (report number [#]). On [date] I sent [company] a written dispute requesting removal of the fraudulent account and enclosed my Identity Theft Report and proof of identity. As of [date], [company] has [not responded / refused to remove the account / requested documents I already provided].

Resolution I am requesting:
Remove the fraudulent account, correct my records, and confirm the correction in writing.

Attached: Identity Theft Report; prior dispute letter; company's response (if any).

After you submit, you will receive a tracking number. Save it in your recovery log along with the date. If the company's response does not resolve the issue, you can provide feedback through the same portal, which keeps the complaint on the company's record.

Credit Freeze Quick Reference

Freeze each agency separately. A freeze is free at every one of them and does not affect your credit score.

> *Phone numbers and mailing addresses change. The web address is the most reliable way in—start there, and treat any printed phone number as a backup to confirm before you rely on it.*

The Three Nationwide Bureaus — Freeze All Three

These are the credit reports lenders check most often. A freeze here is the single highest-impact step against new-account fraud.

Equifax — *credit*

Online: equifax.com/personal/credit-report-services/credit-freeze
Phone: 800-349-9960
Mail: Equifax Security Freeze, P.O. Box 105788, Atlanta, GA 30348-5788

Experian — *credit*

Online: experian.com/freeze/center.html
Phone: 888-397-3742
Mail: Experian Security Freeze, P.O. Box 9554, Allen, TX 75013

TransUnion — *credit*

Online: transunion.com/credit-freeze
Phone: 800-916-8800
Mail: TransUnion, P.O. Box 160, Woodlyn, PA 19094

Three More Worth Freezing

Beyond the big three, these specialty agencies feed decisions about new bank accounts, insurance, and credit. Freezing them closes doors the main bureaus do not cover.

ChexSystems — *new bank and checking accounts*

Online: chexsystems.com (go to Security Freeze)

Note: most banks screen here before opening an account

LexisNexis Risk Solutions — *insurance and identity checks*

Online: consumer.risk.lexisnexis.com/freeze

Phone: 800-456-1244

Mail: LexisNexis Consumer Center, Attn: Security Freeze, P.O. Box 105108, Atlanta, GA 30348-5108

Innovis — *a fourth credit bureau*

Online: innovis.com/personal/securityFreeze

Phone: 800-540-2505

Resource Directory

Every resource here is free and operated by the government or the credit bureaus. Web addresses are the most reliable way in; numbers and pages can change.

Report and Recover

- IdentityTheft.gov — the FTC's reporting and recovery-plan hub; generates your Identity Theft Report.
- ReportFraud.ftc.gov — report scams and fraud to the FTC.
- IC3.gov — the FBI's Internet Crime Complaint Center, including real-estate and title fraud.
- consumerfinance.gov/complaint — the CFPB's complaint portal for stalled disputes with financial companies.

Credit and Freezes

- AnnualCreditReport.com — your free credit reports from all three nationwide bureaus.
- Equifax, Experian, TransUnion — place free credit freezes (see the Credit Freeze Quick Reference).
- ChexSystems, LexisNexis, Innovis — freeze the specialty bureaus that screen new bank and insurance accounts.

Reduce Your Exposure

- OptOutPrescreen.com — stop prescreened credit and insurance offers.
- DoNotCall.gov — register your number with the National Do Not Call Registry.

- Your county recorder or assessor — sign up for free property-recording alerts.

Taxes and Benefits

- IRS.gov — request an Identity Protection PIN and file Form 14039 if your return is affected.
- SSA.gov — review your Social Security earnings record each year for unauthorized use.

Glossary

Plain-language definitions of the terms used throughout this book.

Account takeover. When a criminal seizes control of an account you already have—email, bank, or otherwise—rather than opening a new one in your name.

Business email compromise (BEC). A scam in which an attacker poses as a trusted person, such as an executive or vendor, by email to trick someone into wiring money or sending sensitive data.

CFPB (Consumer Financial Protection Bureau). A federal agency whose online complaint portal can pressure banks, lenders, and credit bureaus to resolve disputes they have ignored.

Credential stuffing. Automated testing of stolen username-and-password pairs across many websites at once, exploiting the habit of reusing the same password.

Credit freeze (security freeze). A free, reversible lock that stops anyone—including you—from opening new credit in your name until you lift it. It does not affect your credit score.

Dark web. Parts of the internet that are not indexed by ordinary search engines, where stolen personal data and credentials are bought and sold.

Data broker. A company that collects, packages, and sells personal information about individuals, usually without their knowledge.

Extended fraud alert. A seven-year alert available to confirmed identity-theft victims who file a report. It also removes you from prescreened-offer lists for five years.

Fair Credit Reporting Act (FCRA). The federal law that governs credit reporting, your right to dispute errors, credit freezes, and the specific protections available to identity-theft victims.

Fraud alert. A notice on your credit file that tells lenders to verify your identity before granting new credit. An initial alert lasts one year and is free.

Home title fraud (deed fraud). Recording a forged deed to transfer ownership of your property to a criminal or a shell company, often targeting paid-off or vacant homes.

IC3 (Internet Crime Complaint Center). The FBI's central hub for reporting internet-enabled crime, found at IC3.gov.

Identity Theft Report. The document generated when you file at IdentityTheft.gov—combined, where required, with a police report—that unlocks your legal rights as a victim.

IP PIN (Identity Protection PIN). A six-digit IRS number, reissued each year, that must accompany your federal tax return and blocks anyone else from filing under your Social Security number.

Knowledge-based authentication (KBA). Identity checks built on "secret" questions like your first pet or childhood street—weak, because the answers are often available in public records.

Medical identity theft. Using your identity or insurance to obtain medical care, prescriptions, or equipment, which can also corrupt your real medical record.

Multi-factor authentication (MFA). Requiring a second proof of identity—a code, an authenticator app, or a physical key—in addition to your password.

New-account fraud. Opening entirely new credit cards, loans, or utility accounts in your name. A credit freeze is the most effective defense.

Phishing. Fraudulent messages—email, text, or otherwise—designed to trick you into revealing credentials or installing malicious software.

Prescreened offers. Unsolicited credit and insurance offers based on your credit data. You can opt out at optoutprescreen.com.

Quiet title action. A lawsuit asking a court to confirm the true owner of a property—the usual remedy for undoing home title fraud.

Section 605B. The provision of the FCRA requiring credit bureaus to block identity-theft information from your file within four business days of a valid report.

SIM swap. Tricking a phone carrier into moving your number to a criminal's device so they can intercept text-message security codes.

Synthetic identity fraud. Combining real and fabricated details—often a real Social Security number with a fake name—to build a new, fictitious identity.

Tax identity theft. Filing a fraudulent tax return using your Social Security number to steal your refund.

Voice cloning. Using artificial intelligence to replicate a person's voice from a short audio sample, often to impersonate a family member or executive.

Your 60-Minute Plan: Completion Checklist

Tear this page out or photograph it. Check each box as you finish. When all five are done, you've closed the doors most attackers rely on.

The Five Core Steps

□ Step 1 — Froze my credit at Equifax, Experian, and TransUnion.

□ Step 2 — Locked down my primary email: new password and multi-factor authentication.

□ Step 3 — Installed a password manager and replaced my reused passwords.

□ Step 4 — Turned on real-time transaction alerts on my financial accounts.

□ Step 5 — Set up property monitoring and started my data-broker opt-outs.

Going Further (optional)

□ Froze the specialty bureaus: ChexSystems, LexisNexis, Innovis.

□ Placed a fraud alert.

□ Requested an IRS Identity Protection PIN.

□ Set a family code word and a second-channel verification rule.

Date completed: ______________________________

APPENDIX

Citations & Sources

The following sources support the statistical claims and data points referenced throughout this book. Opinion-based statements and editorial characterizations are not listed here, as they do not require external citation.

[1] FTC Consumer Sentinel Network Data Book 2024. Total fraud losses and identity theft report counts reflect FTC-reported figures. Available at: consumer.ftc.gov/consumer-sentinel-network

[2] Identity-theft recovery can range from days to many months. In the ITRC's 2024 report, nearly half of victims who contacted ITRC said their issue was **not yet resolved**, and 10% reported dealing with the incident for **six months to one year**. Older FTC research found average resolution time of **30 hours overall** and **60 hours** for more serious new-account/other-fraud cases.

3] FTC historical recovery-time data and ITRC 2024 Consumer Impact Report, on the time required to fully resolve identity theft.

[4] OneRep / Privacy Rights Clearinghouse. The data broker industry encompasses more than 4,000 companies in the U.S. that maintain profiles on virtually every American adult.

[5] Verizon Data Breach Investigations Report (DBIR): "81% of hacking-related breaches leveraged either stolen or weak passwords."

[6] FBI Internet Crime Complaint Center (IC3). "FBI Boston Warns Quit Claim Deed Fraud Is on the Rise." FBI.gov, April 2025. 58,141 victims reported $1.3 billion in real estate fraud losses from 2019–2023. Seniors (60+) accounted for 44% of losses despite representing 19% of complaints.

[7] FTC Consumer Sentinel Network Data Book 2024. Impostor scams reported as top fraud category with over 847,000 complaints.

[8] FTC historical research, cited in BitsFromBytes.com (2026): losses under $5,000 in 82% of cases when discovered within five months; losses over $5,000 in 44% of cases when discovery took six months or longer.

[9] ITRC. "2024 Consumer Impact Report." Consistent with FTC consumer guidance at IdentityTheft.gov.

[10] ITRC. "2024 Consumer Impact Report." 87% of victims felt anxious or worried; 77% felt violated. Cited in Experian.com, July 2024.

[11] ITRC / StationX.net "Identity Theft Statistics 2026." Editorial characterization based on FTC data showing low adoption rates for combined protective measures.

ABOUT THE PUBLISHER

First Advantage Press

First Advantage Press was founded in March 2008 to publish self-help and how-to books for individuals and companies. We address a wide range of topics and strive to make our works actionable and value-creating for every reader.

Our publishing philosophy is straightforward: practical knowledge, clearly presented, with a direct line between what you read and what you do next. Every title we produce is built around that standard.

The 60-Minute Identity Protection Plan is part of our ongoing series addressing the most consequential risks individuals face in a rapidly changing environment. We believe that access to clear, honest, actionable information is one of the most valuable things a publisher can provide.

First Advantage Press | Founded March 2008

FIRSTADVANTAGEPRESS

Publishers of Self-Help and How-To Books

Made in the USA
Coppell, TX
19 June 2026

81947939R00049